Spanish Theater Songs
Baroque and Classical Eras

Carol Mikkelsen, Editor
Translations from Spanish and IPA transcriptions by René Aravena
General Editor of the Alfred Vocal Masterworks Series, John Glenn Paton

Cover art: *Dancing on the Banks of the Manzanares*, 1777,
by Francisco Goya (1746-1828).
Oil on canvas, 272 X 295 cm.
Prado Museum, Madrid, Spain.

This is one of many paintings that Goya produced for the Royal Tapestry Factory
to serve as designs for weaving tapestries that were hung in the royal palaces.

In his old age, Goya acquired a home outside Madrid on the banks of the
Manzanares River.

Table of Contents

Preface

With the growth of interest in Spanish music comes the need to understand its history and development. This anthology of songs and arias from pre-Romantic Spanish theater works is intended to serve this end and, in addition, to present ten concert songs and arias for performance. It contains selections by six noted theater composers of the 1600s through the early 1800s. Many of the songs are appearing in modern print for the first time.

Theater music in the styles represented here played a major role in forming the idiomatic, national style that we recognize as modern Spanish music. This took place through the consolidation of styles from the past, from the countryside and the cities, from the many regions of Spain, and from other countries.

Historical Perspective

No country has a richer song tradition than Spain. This conglomerate of regions, with diverse cultural heritages and languages, has produced a continuous stream of song from earliest recorded Western music history until the present. Prior to Spain's conquest by Muslim invaders from North Africa, known as Moors, in 711 A.D., there existed an extensive body of Christian liturgical music. During the time they ruled the Iberian peninsula, the Moors introduced their musical instruments and theories to Spain; Andalusia became home to centers of Arabic learning and instrument making. Despite the expulsion of the Moors from most of the Iberian peninsula in the late eleventh century, Spanish culture had been irreversibly transformed by almost four centuries of contact with Arabic culture.

The Spanish church was restored in 1080 and adopted the musical forms of Roman Catholicism. Polyphonic church music flourished in Spain through the Middle Ages and Renaissance, culminating in the works of Tomás Luis de Victoria (1548–1611). The Renaissance also saw the rise in popularity of secular songs, classified as either

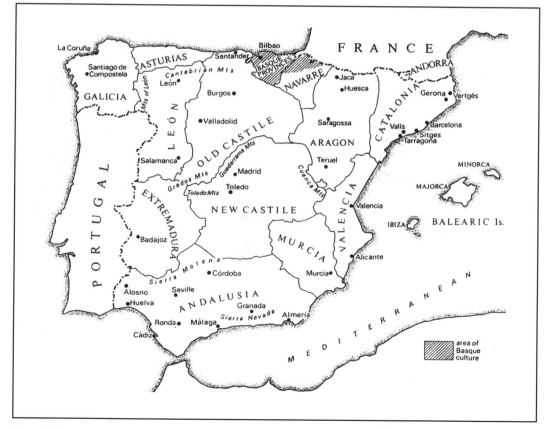

Map of the Regions of Spain. Reprinted from The New Grove Dictionary of Music and Musicians, *edited by Stanley Sadie (London, 1980), by permission.*

Parochial Festival in Valencia, *1862, by A. Rouargue. This engraving of a theatrical performance given in an outdoor courtyard captures the atmosphere and flavor of Spanish music theater, especially of the tonadilla style.*

romances or *villancicos*. This was Spain's "Golden Age" of music, and the accompanied solo song contributed significantly to the epoch's musical greatness.

The *canción* (generic Spanish term for song) continued to be a part of the country's musical life but gave up its dominant role for the next two centuries to theater music. A new kind of solo song, termed *tonada,* made its way into the theater in the 1600s, gaining a new kind of momentum. Spain's loss of political and social dominance during the seventeenth century left it open to invasion by outside forces. The moment was seized by the Italians and their opera, which resulted in an explosion of theater music. Italian opera dominated the musical scene in Spain for a time until a nationalistic reaction occurred. The opposing forces of Italian opera and nationalistic theater music vied for dominance in the hearts of Spaniards for two centuries.

The two major types of Spanish music theater are the *zarzuela* and the *tonadilla escénica*. The zarzuela got its name from festivals of drama and music performed at the palace of La Zarzuela. The palace was a country estate of King Philip IV, having in turn received its name from a bramblebush which grew profusely on the property. This form of musical drama was first written by the poet Pedro Calderón de la Barca (1600–1681). It is characterized by division into two acts and the alternation of singing and dancing with spoken dialogue. The early zarzuelas were of a mythical character and dealt with legendary figures. The transformation from legendary type to a popular one, dealing with real people and situations, occurred in the third quarter of the eighteenth century.

The zarzuela vanished from the Spanish stage in the late 1700s due to the preponderance of Italian opera and the rise in popularity of the tonadilla escénica. The tonadilla escénica, which represented the spirit of the populace of Spain, evolved from the tonadas appended to theatrical pieces. These incidental songs were performed by one person accompanying him/herself on guitar. The song took on such personality that it became a scene with ensuing stage action and often involved more than one character. An independent musical dramatic genre was born. These "little song scenes" soon called for an orchestral accompaniment, which included the guitar, and stretched to approximately twenty minutes in length.

The tonadilla escénica achieved phenomenal success. There were thousands of them written, many preserved in libraries in Spain. Many works enjoyed instant popularity but suffered a brief life span of about seven days. The tonadillas dealt with a wide variety of subjects, nearly all of them depicting typical phases of popular life. The lower strata of society provided models for the characters, most important of which were the swashbuckling men and street ladies of Madrid called *majos* and *majas*. The tonadillas were generally humorous and often satirized conventional patterns of behavior, be it the fashion of Italian opera singers or the majos and majas themselves.

However, by the 1830s the tonadilla had run its course, and opposition to the Italian influence was on the rise. It was toward the middle of the nineteenth century that the resurgent zarzuela really came into its own. This modern zarzuela was of a different nature from the zarzuela of the previous century. The new zarzuelas took over the contemporary subject matter and popular character of tonadillas in two- and three-act entertainments.

The music of the tonadilla marks the emergence of what is referred to as "the Spanish idiom." The style was spread throughout Europe not so much by performances of tonadillas outside of Spain, but rather through the use of tonadilla songs by other composers. Chief among these were the opera and song composers Georges Bizet, Saverio Mercadante, Ernesto Halffter, Enrique Granados, Joaquín Nin and Fernando Obradors.

Song Classifications

Solo pieces in zarzuelas are sometimes called *canción, arieta* or *aria*. The two zarzuela selections in this anthology are being referred to as arias because of their musical character. The remainder of the selections are from tonadillas and are appropriately referred to as songs or *canciones*. These songs often received generic subtitles from their composers, indicating the musical characters of the songs. All subtitles in this volume are particular types of dance-songs. The fourth and sixth entries have no given subtitles. Number four is in the style of an arioso and is being referred to as a canción. The title of number six, "Bailete agitanado," indicates that it is a gypsy dance, but it is non-specific in character. The description, "Bailete-Duetto," indicates that it is a dance-song performed by two people.

Dance-Song Genres

The *tirana* is a classical dance-song from the region of Andalusia. It is of a light-hearted nature in $\frac{3}{8}$ or $\frac{6}{8}$ time. If the song is to be danced, it is performed by a man waving his hat or handkerchief and a woman waving her apron.

The *polo* is also from Andalusia and is one of a family of dance-songs called *cante jondo,* which comes out of the flamenco tradition. The cante jondo, meaning "deep song," may be described as song that expresses a tragic sense of life. The cante jondo style of singing incorporates the use of semi-tones, portamenti, slides, ornate melodic embellishments and repeated notes broken up by appoggiaturas from above and below; this style of ornamentation is believed to have come from Arabic music. The polo is in $\frac{3}{8}$ or $\frac{6}{8}$ meter in a moderate tempo. There are usually rapid coloraturas sung to words such as "Ay."

The *minué* is an imported dance-song, having come from France where it was introduced at the court of Louis XIV about 1650. It is in $\frac{3}{4}$ meter in a moderate tempo.

Composers

Antonio Literes (1673–1747) was a composer for the church and the court, who served the royal chapel in Madrid from 1691 until 1705. His reputation at court was that of a composer of stage music, but only four of his stage works have survived. Three of these are called zarzuelas, although they differ from the traditional form in that the set pieces are in the italianate style. The fourth surviving work is an opera in Spanish but in an Italian musical style. Literes was considered the most gifted composer of his era.

Luis Misón (d.1766), born in Barcelona, began his musical career as a flautist and oboist in the royal chapel in Madrid, where he subsequently became the orchestra conductor. Although many people contributed to the development of the tonadilla, he was one of its most important proponents. He contributed greatly to the formalization of its structure and wrote nearly 100 works. One of his tonadillas, *Una mesonera y un arriero* (1757), serves as a prototype of the genre. He also composed zarzuelas, comic one-acts called *sainete* and Italian *intermezzi.*

Antonio Rodríguez de Hita (ca.1724–1787) was, as Spaniards say, a *madrileño legítimo,* or a legitimate native of Madrid, who grew up in the atmosphere of the *majos* and *majas.* As a composer and theorist he worked both in the sacred and secular arenas. His stage works ran the gamut of styles, ranging from the predominately italianate, mythological zarzuela to folk-influenced pieces. He, together with dramatist Ramón de la Cruz, created the first zarzuela in the popular style. One such work, *Las labradoras de Murcia,* incorporated the use of Spanish folk instruments, which began a trend of such usage. Rodriguez, a progressive, worked to create a native, or popular, Spanish opera.

Pablo Esteve y Grimau (1730–1794), conductor of the Teatro de la Cruz in Madrid, was one of the most successful and highly regarded composers of tonadillas. He composed more than four hundred of them, writing the texts for many. This proud Catalan musician fearlessly tried to gain respect for himself and other tonadilla composers, since some people considered their work of lesser artistic value. He was impeded in this effort by an incident with a famous singer, known as "La Caramba," which landed him in jail for allowing satires against society women in his stage productions. He translated and adapted operas by foreign composers for production in Spain, often inserting some of his own music.

Blas de Laserna (1751–1816) is the second great name of *tonadilleros,* a name given to composers of tonadillas. He composed around seven hundred tonadillas, at his height being contracted to write sixty-three a year by one impresario. In addition, he wrote other forms of stage works including zarzuelas and sainetes. In 1790 he succeeded Esteve as conductor at the Teatro de la Cruz. Laserna was fiercely nationalistic, resisting any Italian musical influences, and even proposed founding a school to preserve authentic Spanish music. Towards the end of his career, because of financial reasons, he was forced to adopt the Italian musical vogue in order to have his works produced.

Manuel del Pópolo Vicente García (1775–1832) is considered to be the last of the tonadilleros. He began his career as a singer and composer of tonadillas. He was quite possibly the most influential musical person of Spanish descent during his lifetime; as Rossini's "favorite tenor," he originated many operatic roles and was a leading vocal pedagogue. Sevillian by birth, he brought his Andalusian charm, passionate singing style and "Spanish idiom" to Europe and North America. Each of his two remarkable polos contained in this anthology served as inspiration for a significant number of musical works, both vocal and instrumental. (For more works of García in French and Spanish, see *Songs and Duets of García, Malibran and Viardot,* ed. Patricia Adkins Chiti, Alfred Publishing Co., 1997.)

Vocal Ornamentation

Although much has been written about vocal ornamentation in Italian, French and German music during the period covered in this volume, much less can be said with certainty about ornamentation in Spanish music. Some of the songs in this book were composed in imitation of the predominant Italian style; these songs can safely be ornamented just like Italian arias of the same time. Songs that have their origin in Spanish dance rhythms may nevertheless be embellished with ornaments that were common property of all other countries in their time. Accordingly, the editor has supplied most of the songs in this book with suggested ornaments. Such ornaments always appear in small notes to emphasize that they are editorial suggestions and not creations of the composers. The singer may omit them, use them, or invent others to replace them.

The polos composed by Manuel García present quite a different situation: they are so brilliantly virtuosic that it is not necessary to add embellishment. Furthermore, García used ornaments that are never heard in Italian music; they come from García's native region, Andalusia, where Moorish presence was strong until 1492. It is not clear whether the florid Andalusian vocal style owes more to the Moors or to the gypsies.

Portrait of Manuel García, *by Francisco Jose de Goya y Lucientes.*
Bequest of John T. Spaulding
Courtesy, Museum of Fine Arts, Boston.

About This Edition

This anthology is intended to be not only a scholarly and interesting presentation of a body of relatively unknown vocal music, but also a useful pedagogical resource. For this reason the accompanying historic and linguistic information is provided.

For many Americans, singing in Spanish is an easy task. Spanish is a first language for many Americans and is the favorite foreign language taught in this country's schools. Since the songs in this anthology are by composers from Spain, it is recommended that Castillian pronunciation be used. This volume includes a guide to Castillian, an International Phonetic Alphabet key and a phonetic transcription of each entry.

Extensive information about the music, composers and singing style is included in order to present a historic perspective for this relatively obscure music. Accompanying each song and aria are a literal transla-tion and an idiomatic translation. In addition, a "Poetic Idea" is given as a guide to the study of the song or aria. "Background Information," provided for each entry, includes a few pertinent facts about the source of the piece, its genre and its historical significance.

The sources used in the compilation of material for this edition have been musicological publications from Spain and France that have been difficult if not impossible to buy on the market in English language countries. Piano transcriptions of original orchestral accompaniments found in these publications are being used, and credit is given to the transcribers/editors. Some errors in the sources have been corrected without comment. Further editorial suggestions, clearly identified as such, have been added to aid in learning and interpreting the songs.

Acknowledgments

The publication of this anthology of Spanish songs would not have been possible without the assistance of many people. Chief among them is John Glenn Paton, whose initial excitement over the proposal and constant encouragement and supervision throughout the process led to the book's successful completion. Dr. René Aravena of California State University, Los Angeles, added not only his profound knowledge of Spanish phonetics but also his imaginative cultural insights to questions of language and custom. A special thanks goes to Mary Kate Karr, Editorial Administrator of the Vocal Masterworks Series, for her skill and patience in working with this novice editor. It is a great fortune indeed to have Alfred Publishing Co. publish the book.

Much of the initial research for this book was done here at Valdosta State University. I'm indebted to the Odum Library Staff, in particular, Denise Montgomery, and to members of the faculty of the Modern & Classical Languages Department. Dr. Sandra Walker, Department Head, provided significant help with translations of song texts and source material in Spanish. Translations of French resource material were made by Lee Bradley, Chevalier dans l'Ordre des Palmes Académiques, Assistant Professor, Valdosta State University.

Carol Mikkelsen
Valdosta, Georgia

The cover of Teatro lírico español, *edited by Felipe Pedrell (1841–1922) and published by Canuto Berea and Company at La Coruña in 1898. This monumental anthology is the source of several songs included here. Ambitious as a composer, Pedrell also published musicological writings in Spanish, Catalan and French. Enrique Granados (1867–1916) studied composition with Pedrell, who influenced many composers to honor their Spanish heritage and express it in their works.*

Confiado jilguerillo

from *Acis y Galatea* (1708)

[ásis i ɣalatéa]

Antonio Literes

(1673–1747)

konfiáðo xilɣeríʎo
1 Confiado jilguerillo,
Trusting   little-linnet,

míɾa kómo‿importúna
2 mira como   importuna,
see   how   untimely

de twestáðo priméɾo
3 de tu estado primero,
from your place   first

te ðeriβó‿   el amór i la fortúna
4 te derribó   el amor y la fortuna,
you were-pushed-down-(by)—love and—fortune,

jel βjénto ke tan ufáno presumíste
5 y el   viento que tan ufano presumiste,
and the wind   that so   proudly you-assumed

aún no le‿aʎáste   kwándo le perðíste.
6 aún no le hallaste   cuando le perdiste.
still not it you-did-find when   it you-lost.

si   ðe ráma‿en ráma
7 Si   de   rama en rama,
When from bough to bough,

si   ðe flor en flor
8 si   de flor en flor,
when from flower to flower

íβas   saltándo
9 ibas   saltando,
you-were hopping,

βuʎéndoi̯   kantándo
10 bullendo   y   cantando,
making-noise and singing,

ditʃóso kjen   áma
11 ¡dichoso quién   ama
"Happy one-who loves

las ánsjas   ðe‿amór
12 las ansias   de amor!
the yearnings of love,

las íras   ðe‿amór
13 las iras   de amor!
the angers of love!"

aðβjérte ke‿ aprísa
14 Advierte que aprísa
Notice   how quickly

es ʎánto   la rísa
15 es llanto   la risa
is weeping the laughter

jel   gústo   ðolór ai̯ai̯
16 y el gusto   dolor. ¡Ay, ay!
and the pleasure grief.   Alas!

Poetic idea: "Innocent songbird, you used to sing about the pleasure of love, but you see how quickly it can change to grief."

This aria is sung by the beautiful water nymph Galatea in the "heroic zarzuela" *Acis y Galatea.* Galatea, singing to a linnet or goldfinch, reflects on how the bird has been unseated by love from its lofty place atop a tree.

The work is called heroic or legendary because of its mythological subject matter. According to legend, Acis, the lover of Galatea, is killed by his rival, Polyphemus, who also loves Galatea. Upon his death, Acis is transformed into a river.

Background: *Acis y Galatea* was premiered at the Royal Palace in Madrid in honor of King Philip V's birthday. After the premiere of this partly sung, two-act zarzuela, it entered the repertory of the public theatres in Madrid and became possibly the most successful zarzuela of the first half of the 18th century. In the original cast the roles of Acis and Galatea, as well as all but three members of the cast, were sung by women. Literes, much influenced by Italian opera, borrowed many musical features from that style. The Italian aria forms, mostly in the da capo format with recitatives, were juxtaposed with set pieces in the Spanish style.

A setting of "*Confiado jilguerillo*" by Joaquín Nin is found in the first volume of *Quatorze Airs anciens d'auteurs espagnols,* entitled "*Aria de Acis y Galatea.*" Fernando Obradors has an elaborate setting of the aria with an extended, bravura cadenza. Entitled "*Confiado jilguerillo,*" it is found in Volume II of *Canciones clásicas españolas.*

Sources: (1) *Teatro lírico español . . . ,* Vol. 2, Felipe Pedrell (La Coruña, 1898), pp. 1–6. Microfilm copy (Shelf No. 772), Library of Congress, Washington, D.C.

(2) Reprinted, omitting the recitative, in: "*La musique en*

Espagne," Rafael Mitjana in *Encyclopédie de la musique et dictionnaire du Conservatoire,* Part I, Vol. 4, Lavignac-Laurencie (Paris, 1920), pp. 2111–2113.

(3) Reprinted in: *Cancionero musical popular español,* Vol. 3, Felipe Pedrell (Valls, 1918–1922), pp. 85–93.

Pedrell's edition, for voice and piano, is based on the original score preserved in the archives of the Ayuntamiento of Madrid.

Original key: G minor, with a signature of one flat. For soprano, two violins and continuo. The recitative was accompanied by strings. Some incomplete chords in the score would have been completed by a keyboard instrument, and so they have been completed here accordingly. An exception is the first half of measure 8, where, in the score, the indication *tasto solo* means that there should be no harmony. Suggested embellishments in the da capo section of the aria have also been given here.

In the aria the violin parts are printed in normal notes; cue-sized notes indicate additions by the editor.

Confiado jilguerillo

José de Cañizares

Antonio Literes
Transcribed by Felipe Pedrell

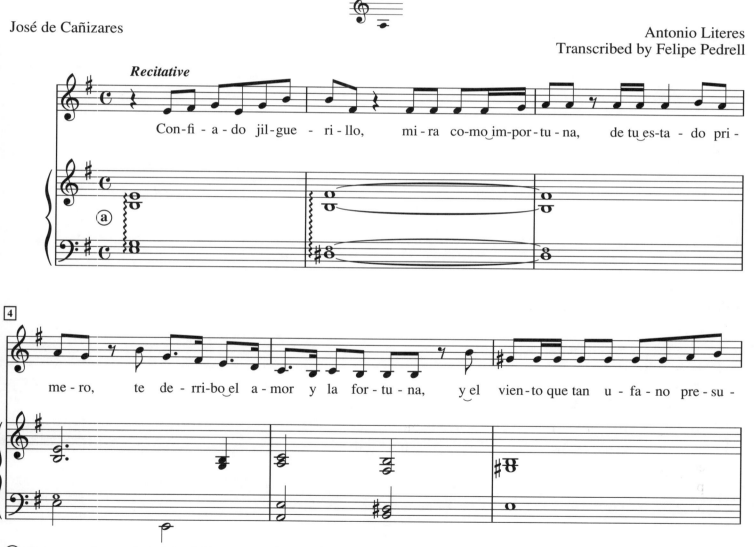

ⓐ Because a piano or harpsichord does not sustain as well as the original stringed instruments, the accompanist is encouraged to add tones and repeat chords as needed to support the singer in the recitative.

Idiomatic translation: Trusting little linnet, see how untimely love and fortune made you fall from that high place, and the wind, that you once so proudly

mis - te, aún no le ha-llas-te cuan-do le per-dis - te.

tasto solo

[Andante, ♩ = 90–96]

mp

cresc.

decresc.

ⓑ

Si de ra-ma en ra - ma, si de flor en flor,

mf

i - bas sal - tan-do, bu - llen-do y can - tan - do, ¡di - cho-so quién

mf

ⓑ Play as two eighth notes.

took for granted, is now lost, never to be found. From bough to bough, from flower to flower, you used to flit, bustle and sing: "Lucky are those

a - ma las an - sias de a - mor!   I - bas sal -

tan - do,   i - bas sal - tan - do, bu - llen - do y can -

tan   - - - - - - - - -

do, ¡di - cho - so quién a - ma las an - sias de a - mor! I - bas   sal - tan - do,

who find pleasure in longing for love!"

"Lucky are those who love the fury of love." Notice how quickly laughter turns to tears and pleasure to grief.

© Play either the full-sized notes or the small notes, not both.

Ya canta el ave

from *Los jardineros* (1761)

[los xarðineɾos]

Luis Misón
(1727–1766)

Alcino [alθíno]:

1
ja kánta el áve
Ya canta el ave,
Now sings the bird,

2
bjéne la‿auɾóɾa
viene la aurora,
comes the dawn,

3
i se lo ðóɾa
y se lo dora
and to it makes-golden

4
tóðo el βerxél
todo el vergel.
all the garden.

5
si aβɾá salíðo
Si habrá salido
If she-has come out,

6
mi dwéɲo‿ermóso
mi dueño hermoso,
my mistress fair,

7
ke peɾeθóso
¡qué perezoso,
how lazy,

8
fin i kɾuél
fin y cruel!
shrewd and cruel!

9
deθíðme rósas
Decidme, rosas,
Tell-me, roses

10
deθíðme fwéntes
decidme, fuentes,
tell-me, fountains,

11
deθíðme tɾónkos
decidme, troncos,
tell-me, tree-trunks,

12
deθíð klaβéles
decid, claveles,
tell-me, carnations,

13
si‿a βeníðo mas ʧíto
si ha venido, ¡mas chito!
if (she)-has come, but silence!

14
pwes ja se‿aðβjérte
pues ya se advierte
because already one can-notice,

15
en kestán tóðos βéʎos
en que están todos bellos,
in that are all beautiful,

16
kéʎa está‿auɡsénte
que ella está ausente.
that she is absent.

Doris [dóris]:

17
ja tóðo el βáʎe
Ya todo el valle
Already all the valley

18
la luθ esmálta
la luz esmalta,
the light paints,

19
jel áβe sálta
y el ave salta
and the bird jumps

20
ðe flor en flor
de flor en flor.
from flower to flower.

21
si el dwéɲo mío
Si el dueño mío
If the lord mine

22
sea‿antiθipáðo
se ha anticipado,
himself has come-earlier,

23
kɾwel a‿estáðo
cruel ha estado
cruel he-has been

24
kon el mi amór
con el mi amor . . .
with — my love.

25
si‿a βeníðo mas θjélos
si ha venido, ¡mas cielos!
if he-has arrived, but heavens!

26
kes lo ke‿áʎo
¿Qué es lo que hallo?
What is it that I-see?

27
ja‿enkontɾó mi ðeskúiðo
Ya encontró mi descuido
Already he-met my carelessness

28
kon el kwiðáðo
con el cuidado.
with — carefulness.

Poetic idea: "Tell me, roses; tell me, fountains; tell me, trees; tell me, carnations, if she (he) has arrived."

This song is sung by the young lovers Alcino and Doris at the opening of the pastoral tonadilla *The Gardeners.* Alcino, who arrives in the garden at dawn, looks for clues to tell him if his beloved has arrived as yet (verse 1). Doris appears in the garden a moment later, hoping that she is the first to arrive.

Background: Luis Misón, once thought to have been the originator of the tonadilla, contributed greatly to its success and development. *Los jardineros* was premiered about ten years after the emergence of the genre. In the early years of development, the tonadilla was performed as an appendage to a larger dramatic work. In this case the larger drama was an *auto sacramental,* a religious play, entitled *De lo que va ó el hombre de Dios,* given for the feast of Corpus Christi.

Los jardineros was written for two specific singers, María Ladvenant and Mariana Alcázar. The performance of a male role by a female singer was a common occurence in Spanish stage works, particularly those of a serious nature.

An interesting note about performance practices of this era is the placement of the orchestra behind the scenery. Following a 1765 royal decree, which abolished the autos, tonadillas were performed independently and orchestras were placed in front of the stage.

This song can be sung either as a duet, as it was written, or as a solo, with a male or female voice singing either or both verses. *Dueño* is translated as either "lord" or "mistress." The gender specific phrase (verse 1) *"ella está"* can be changed to *"el está"* for a female singer.

Line 6: *mi dueño hermoso* means "my fair lady." The use of a masculine noun to designate the beloved woman appears in many poetic texts.

Line 8: *fin* is probably short for *fino,* "shrewd," but the meaning is unclear.

Lines 14–16: *pues . . . ausente* says by implication that if Doris were present, the garden would no longer look beautiful in comparison with her.

Line 17: Apparently, Alcino has hidden before Doris enters from another direction and looks for him.

Line 23: *cruel,* sung here in one syllable, simply expresses her annoyance at the thought that Alcino may have arrived ahead of her. Each lover hoped to demonstrate love by arriving in the garden first.

Line 26: Doris sees Alcino and knows that her "carelessness" in arriving tardily has been outdone by his "carefulness" in arriving early.

Source: *Music in Eighteenth Century Spain,* Mary Neal Hamilton (Urbana, IL, 1937), pp. 76–79.

Original key: A minor. For two sopranos and orchestra, consisting of two violins, two flutes, horn, bass-viol and clavichord.

Aire de Minué, "song in minuet rhythm," is the tempo marking at the head of the orchestral introduction, which serves as an overture to the tonadilla. It is abbreviated here from the original length of 21 measures.

Note: The parallel chord movement in measures 38–40 is forbidden in the rules of classical harmony, but it sounds both attractive and dramatic to ears that are accustomed to the guitar idiom. These measures may be sung freely, resuming the tempo at measure 42.

Ya canta el ave

Luis Misón
Transcribed by Mary Neal Hamilton

[Tempo di Minuetto, ♩ = 80–88]

Idiomatic translation: (Alcino): Birds are singing, the day is dawning, and the whole garden seems made of gold. If my fair mistress is already out, how lazy, shrewd and cruel I have been!

(Doris): Now the whole valley is painted with light, now birds are flitting from flower to flower. If my beloved has come earlier, he has been cruel with my love.

(Alcino):   Tell me, roses, tell me, fountains, tell me, trees, tell me, carnations, if she has come, but hush! I can tell
that she is not here, because you are still beautiful.

(Doris):   Tell me, roses, tell me, fountains, tell me, trees, tell me, carnations, if he has come, but heavens! He has
already anticipated me with thoughtfulness.

De pena, de susto

from *Las Labradoras de Murcia* (1769)

[las laβraðóras ðe múrθja]

Ramón de la Cruz

Antonio Rodríguez de Hita
(ca. 1725–1787)

de péna,   de sústo
1 **De pena,   de susto,**
   Of sorrow, of fear,

faʎéθe mi βíða
2 **fallece mi vida,**
   perishes my life,

θerkána͜ oρrimíða
3 **cercana oprimida,**
   close   oppressed

del   último mal
4 **del   último mal.**
   by-the ultimate evil.

o θjélo ke míras
5 **O cielo que miras**
   Oh heaven that sees

mi mal   riɣoróso
6 **mi mal   rigoroso,**
   my suffering cruel,

reméðja pjaðóso
7 **remedia piadoso**
   remedy   mercifully

mi swérte fatál.
8 **mi suerte fatal.**
   my luck   fatal.

Poetic idea: "I feel hopeless in this situation. I pray for mercy and a change of my fate."

Teresa, a young woman in love, sings this aria in the second act of *The Workingwomen of Murcia*. Teresa expresses her fear as she awaits her lover at a favorite meeting place, as well as her confidence in the divine grace which will put an end to her sorrows.

The plot centers on Don Vicente, foreman of a silk-worm farm in the region of Murcia, and his daughter, Teresa. Vicente is a refugee from the law, having been falsely accused of a murder. Teresa is in conflict because she is in love with the actual murderer, Narciso. The plot resolves happily when the truth emerges and Narciso is officially exonerated of the murder that he committed.

Background: *Las Labradoras de Murcia* belongs to the popular zarzuela genre and stands out as the masterpiece of the Spanish lyric theater in the 1700s. This is due in part to the successful way the composer and the librettist, the prominent dramatist Ramón de la Cruz, linked Spanish folklore tradition with Italian opera conventions. The aria *"De pena, de susto"* displays italianate melodic and expressive qualities within the da capo aria form.

Spanish folk music influences several scenes in the zarzuela, most of all the finale of the first act, which takes place in the silk nursery during a thunderstorm. According to a local superstition, silkworms die of fright upon hearing thunder, so workers attempt to cover nature's rumblings by singing, playing musical instruments and dancing. Rodríguez accomplished this by having the orchestra depict the sounds of the storm while the characters on stage sing and accompany themselves with guitars, mandolins, drums and castanets, while they dance the *jota murciana*.

This zarzuela was revived in 1896 in observance of the centenary of the death of Ramón de la Cruz.

Line 3. The rest which interrupts *oprimida* expresses breathlessness or sobbing. The diphthong must be pronounced before the rest, with [a] prolonged more than [o].

Sources: (1) *Don Ramón de la Cruz y sus obras,* Emilio Cotarelo y Mori (Madrid, 1899), musical supplement, pp. 5–8; transcription from the original score found in the Municipal Library in Madrid.

(2) Reprinted in: *"La Musique en Espagne,"* Rafael Mitjana in *Encyclopédie de la musique et dictionnaire du Conservatoire,* Part I, Vol. 4, Lavignac-Laurencie (Paris, 1920), pp. 2164–2166.

Original key: A minor. For soprano and orchestra, scored for violins, violas, celli, basses, two flutes, two oboes, two horns and two trumpets. Source (1) gives a longer instrumental postlude.

A suggested cadenza at the end of the middle section and a few melodic embellishments to the da capo section of the aria are given here by the editor. Dynamic markings from source (1) are printed full size; dynamics added by the editor are reduced in size.

De pena, de susto

Ramón de la Cruz

Antonio Rodríguez de Hita
Transcribed by Emilio Cotarelo y Mori

Idiomatic translation: Full of sorrow, full of fear, my life is perishing; I am a prisoner of the ultimate evil.

O God, you who see my cruel suffering, in mercy change my deadly fate.

ⓐ Cadenza suggested by the editor.

ⓑ The pianist may play the small notes if the singer also ornaments.

¡Alma, sintamos!

from *Garrido de luto por la muerte de Caramba* (1781)

[garíðo ðe lúto por la mwérte ðe karámba]

Pablo Esteve
(1730–1794)

	álma	sintámos	óxos	ʎoráð
1	**¡Alma,**	**sintamos!**	**¡Ojos,**	**llorad**
	Soul,	let-us-grieve!	Eyes,	weep

	a	mi	karámba	ke	murjó	ja
2	**a**	**mi Caramba**		**que**	**murió**	**ya!**
	for	my Caramba,		who	died	just-now!

	ai̯	poβreθíta	tóða	bondáð
3	**¡Ay,**	**pobrecita!**	**Toda**	**bondad**
	Alas,	poor-little-girl!	All	goodness,

	ke	no	tenía	pekáðo	βenjál
4	**que**	**no**	**tenía**	**pecado**	**venial.**
	that	not	had	sin	venial.

Poetic idea: "Weep with me for the good woman who has just died!"

Both text and music of this song express deep grief by every means possible. Minor mode, stately tempo and sobbing grace notes combine with chromatic harmonies and throbbing bass notes to touch our hearts.

The irony is that the woman being mourned is not really dead. Every member of the original audience knew that and sat eagerly anticipating the star's entrance on stage.

Background: María Antonia Fernández came to Madrid from Andalusia with its gypsy tradition of fiery dancing and passionate singing, later called *cante flamenco.* Soon after her arrival she acquired a nickname, La Caramba. She was singing in a tonadilla with her favorite partner, Miguel Garrido, and teasing him about his small size. Her song ended with the exclamation *"Caramba!,"* which is still in common use to mean something like "dear me" or "goodness!" Garrido became known as Carambón, and Caramba's nickname was also given to her favorite fashion item, an oversized brightly colored hairbow, which became a fad in Madrid.

In 1781 Fernández shocked her fans by retiring from the stage to devote herself to marriage. Fortunately for her audiences, she left her husband after only a few weeks. For her return to the stage she approached Pablo Esteve, who had already written a number of tonadillas that exploited the bantering of

Caramba and Carambón. Esteve produced *Garrido in Mourning for the Death of Caramba,* in which Garrido mourns for his deceased love until she suddenly reappears and they joyfully pick up their partnership where they had left it off. So her return from "death" on stage was also her return from "retirement" to her public.

Caramba's passionate singing and dancing style was matched by her outrageous behavior. In 1782 she sued Esteve for not writing other tonadillas for her as popular as *Garrido de luto . . . .*

In later music double appoggiaturas were often performed before the beat, but both double and triple appoggiaturas on the beat are recommended in *Introduction to the Art of Playing on the Piano Forte* by Muzio Clementi [London: Clementi, et al., 1801]. They are shown here as 32nd notes, but they may be played even faster if it is practical to do so.

Joaquín Nin has a setting of *"¡Alma, sintamos!"* in the first volume of *Quatorze Airs anciens d'auteurs espagnols.*

Sources: (1) *Teatro lírico español . . . ,* Vol. 2, Felipe Pedrell (La Coruña, 1898), pp. 12–14. Microfilm copy (Shelf No. 772), Library of Congress, Washington, D.C.

(2) Reprinted in: *"La musique en Espagne,"* Rafael Mitjana in *Encyclopédie de la musique et dictionnaire du Conservatoire,* Part I, Vol. 4, Lavignac-Laurencie (Paris, 1920), pp. 2237, 2238.

Original key: B minor. For tenor and orchestra.

¡Alma, sintamos!

Pablo Esteve

Pablo Esteve
Transcribed by Felipe Pedrell

Andante espressivo [♪ = 70–76]

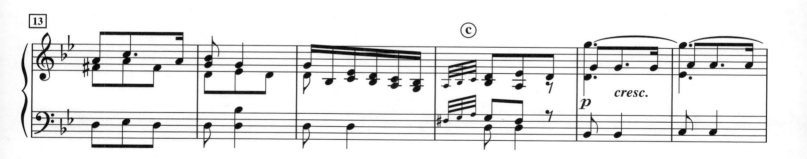

(a) Perform all double appoggiaturas on the beat:

(b) Perform all triple appoggiaturas on the beat:

(d) Perform all double appoggiaturas on the beat:

Al -ma___ sin -

Idiomatic translation: Soul, let us grieve! Eyes, let us weep! My loving Caramba has died! Ay, poor girl, she was all goodness and never committed a sin.

¡O - jos,_ llo - rad_ a mi Ca-ram-ba que mu-rió_ ya,_

a mi Ca-ram - ba que mu-rió ya,_ que mu - rió_ ya,_

p cresc.

que mu - rió_ ya!_

Tirana del cangrejo

from *Los celos iguales* (1782?)

[los θélos iɣwáles]

Pablo Esteve
(1730–1794)

1
afírman   ke ðel maríðo
Afirman   que del marido
They-affirm that of-the husband

2
es enemíɣo̯ el kanɣréxo
es enemigo el cangrejo,
is enemy   the crab,

3
i   ɟo díɣo kes   mentíra
y   yo digo que es mentira
and I say that is a-lie

4
pwes ke le permíte ðéntro
pues que le permite dentro.
because — (it) is-allowed inside.

5
ai̯ kanɣrexíʎo tʃikíto
¡Ay! cangrejillo chiquito,
Ay, little-crab   small,

6
ai̯ kanɣrexíʎo ðel   mar
¡ay! cangrejillo del   mar,
ay, little-crab   from-the sea,

7
míra ke̯ ánda   la tirána
mira que anda   la tirana
look how is-walking the tirana

8
al láðo ðel   farfalá
al lado del   farfalá.
— close to-the ruffles.

9
ben aká   kanɣréxo
¡Ven acá,   cangrejo,
Come over-here, crab!

10
kanɣréxo̯ aká βen
cangrejo, acá ven!
crab,   here come-over!

11
ke   ðéntʃo ðel pétʃo
Que   dentro del pecho
so-that inside of-the bosom

12
ɟo te̯ okultaré
yo te   ocultaré.
I you will-hide.

13
peɾo kwénta   kanɣrexíto
Pero cuenta,   cangrejito,
But make-sure, little crab,

14
ke no me mwérðas kon el
que no me muerdas con él.
that not me you-bite with it[claw].

15
a   kanɣrexíʎo, kwénta   kon morðér
¡Ah, cangrejillo, cuenta   con morder!
Ah, little-crab,   make-sure of biting!

16
o kwántos tóman la βéka
Oh cuántos toman la beca
Oh, how-many get   the stipend

17
en maðríð ðe kolexjáles
en Madrid de colegiales;
in Madrid as school-boys;

18
los únos en los koléxjos
los unos en los colegios,
— some in the high-schools,

19
los ótros en ótras pártes
los otros en otras partes.
the others in other places.

Poetic idea: "Hey, little crab, I'll hide you if you won't bite. No, bite all you want!"

Something is going on here, but the singer doesn't want to come out and say exactly what she means. Everyone knows that crabs can bite, move sideways in a sneaky manner, and hide in tight places, but what could it mean that the crab might be a husband's enemy?

When she mentions in the second stanza that some high school boys get their education in school and some get it in other places, her meaning becomes clear enough for an alert audience to draw a connection and understand the symbolism of the "dear little crab."

Background: *"Tirana of the Crab"* comes from *The Equal Jealousies,* another in the series of tonadillas that Esteve wrote for the popular performers known as Caramba and Carambón. Their story was told in the commentary to *"¡Alma, sintamos!"*

The tirana is a lighthearted dance-song usually in $\frac{3}{8}$ or $\frac{6}{8}$ time, characterized by syncopated rhythmic patterns. The lyrics are usually in the form of *coplas,* verses, and *estribillo,* refrain, and were often risqué. Spoken lines between the verses and at the end of the song were also common. Most tonadillas in the 1780s ended with tiranas.

Source: *Teatro lírico español . . . ,* Vol. 2, Felipe Pedrell (La Coruña, 1898), pp. 35–37. Microfilm copy (Shelf No. 772), Library of Congress, Washington, D.C.

Original key: F Major. For voice and orchestra. The frequent changes of dynamics are in the original score.

Tirana del cangrejo

Pablo Esteve

Pablo Esteve
Transcription by Felipe Pedrell

Allegro [♪ = 138–160]

1. A - fir - man que del__ ma - ri - do es e - ne - mi -
2. Oh cuán - tos to - man__ la be - ca en Ma - drid de

go el__ can - gre - jo, y yo di - go qué es men - ti - ra pues
co - le - gia - les; los u - nos en los__ co - le - gios, los

Idiomatic translation: (1) Some say that the crab is a husband's worst enemy. But, I say: that's not true, 'cause
(2) Many students get a stipend in the city of Madrid. Some will get it in the schools,

26

que le per - mi - te den - tro. ¡Ay! can - gre - ji - llo chi - qui - to,
o - tros en o - tras par - tes.

33

(a) ¡ay! can - gre - ji - llo del mar, mi - ra___ que an - da la ti -
(b)

40

(c) ra - na al la - do del far - fa - lá. ¡Ven a - cá, can - gre - jo, can -

47

gre - jo, a - cá ven! Que den - tro del pe - cho yo te o - cul - ta - ré. Pe - ro

(a) (b) Perform the acciaccaturas quickly and before the beat.
(c) Perform as two equal eighth notes.

(1) he is allowed inside. Ay, tiny little crab, little crab from the sea! Look how the tirana makes the petticoats go!
    Come over here, my crab, I will hide you in my bosom. Just
(2) others in some other places.

don't bite me, little crab, Ah, little crab, bite as much as you want!

Bailete agitanado

from *Los majos reñidos* (1782?)

[los maxos reɲiðos]

Pablo Esteve
(1730–1794)

1
θa θa θa
Za, za, za,
Za, za, za,

2
álθa kukukurutíta
alza, cucucurrutita.
get up, cucucurrutita.

3
bája kukukurutíto
Vaya, cucucurrutito.
Go, cucucurrutito.

4
ai̯ θa ke mas θa tʃis tʃis
Ay, za, que más za, chis, chis,
Ay, za, what more za, chis, chis,

5
ai̯ θa ke mas θa tʃas tʃas
ay, za, que más za, chas, chas.
ay, za, what more za, chas, chas.

6
bámos ʎéβa kompás el pretérito
Vamos lleva a compás el pretérito.
Let's-go, keep in rhythm the preterit

7
i tu kon álma̯el imperfékto
Y tu, con alma el imperfecto.
and you with soul the imperfect.

8
ai̯ θa ke βjéne ke tórna
Ay, za, que viene, que torna.
Ay, za, that comes, that goes-back.

9
ai̯ θa ke βwélβe ke βa
Ay, za, que vuelve, que va.
Ay, za, that returns, that goes-ahead.

10
ai̯ θa ke si no le kóxe
Ay, za, que si no le coge,
Ay, za, that if not him you-grab,

11
ai̯ θa te seskapaɾá
Ay, za, te se escapará.
Ay, za, from-you it will-escape.

12
—θa kíta áʎa
—Za... ¡Quita allá!
Za... Stop that!

13
—ke tjénes
—¿Qué tienes?
What is-the-matter-with-you?

14
— ke me fálta̯el materjál
—¿Qué me falta el material.
That I lack the material.

15
—pwes ixíta, akaβóse el xornál
—Pues, hijita, acabóse el jornal.
Well, girl, finished-is the money.

Poetic idea: This seemingly non-sensical set of lyrics amounts to a verbal sparring match between the famous singer Caramba and her partner, Carambón, in *The Quarrelling Majos*. There is a lively dance going on while the couple tease and toss poetic barbs at each other. A disguised jab is achieved through the use of the words "preterit" (past) and "imperfect," which denote verb tenses as well as states of being.

In the 1700s all the craftsmen of Madrid were referred to as *majos.* Some of them were quick-witted, especially the women, or *majas.* They liked to spend their money on their gaudy attire, and they were characterized by boldness and insolence, even licentiousness. There were also what Ramón de la Cruz called *majos decentes,* who were more moderate in their lifestyle and dress and used to rise above their class. Some of the charm of Spanish musical theater in this period comes from the skill with which the authors captured the metaphoric language and dry wit of the majos, with which they both imitated and satirized the upper classes.

Lines 1–2: *Za* is the second syllable of *¡alza!,* a typical outcry of the non-dancing participants during a flamenco dance performance. Among gypsies, the word would be pronounced [árθa].

Line 14: *material* is deliberately vague; it might mean booze, among other things.

Although written for two singers, *"Bailete agitanado"* can be performed as a solo by cutting the sections with dialogue (mm. 32–49 and mm. 70–79).

Background: *Bailete agitanado* means "gypsy dance," suggesting a faster tempo than that of the tiranas in this book.

Los majos reñidos premiered in the same year as *Los celos iguales,* and was another showpiece for Caramba and Garrido. In 1785 Caramba gave up singing for a career as a penitent, making amends for her former lifestyle.

The three numbers by Esteve in this book could be programed together as a mini-cycle by two singers who can recreate the personalities of the original performers.

Source: *Teatro lírico español,* Vol. 2, Felipe Pedrell (La Coruña, 1898), pp. 38–41. Microfilm copy (Shelf No. 772), Library of Congress, Washington, D.C.

Original key: A Major. For soprano, tenor and orchestra.

Maja and Cloaked Men, *1777, detail, by Francisco Jose de Goya y Lucientes (1746–1828). Oil on canvas, 275 x 190 cm. Prado Museum, Madrid, Spain.*

Like the painting shown on the front cover, this painting was produced for the Royal Tapestry Factory to serve as a design for a woven tapestry to be hung in the royal palace.

In 1766 a royal minister influenced the king to issue decrees that forbade the majos to wear wide sombreros and long capes because they made it too easy for thieves to hide their faces while escaping from the police. Violent riots broke out and lasted for days until the king had to rescind his decrees. The minister was fired and replaced by a cleverer one, who had the king decree that wide sombreros and long capes would be the official uniform of hangmen. In this way the traditional garb naturally went out of fashion. This painting shows the smaller hats and shorter capes of the new fashion.

Bailete agitanado

Pablo Esteve

Pablo Esteve
Transcription by Felipe Pedrell

Allegro vivace [♩. = 76–84]

He / Za, za, za, al - za, al - za, cu - cu - cu - rru - ti - ta. ___ Za, za, za, va - ya,

She

(a) Perform double appoggiaturas on the beat, as:

Idiomatic translation: Get up, cucurrutita!

Go, cucurrutito! Ay, za, more, za, chis chis! Ay, za, more, za, chas, chas! *Come on, keep up with the preterit!*

She *(spoken)*

Y tú, con alma el imperfecto.

Both

Ay, za, que vie - ne, que tor - na. Ay, za, que vuel - ve que va.

Ay, za, que si no le co - ge, Ay, za, te

And you, put your soul into the imperfect! Ay, za, it's coming and going. Ay, za, if you don't grab it,

you'll let it escape. *Za, stop that! What's the matter? I ran out of it. Well, girl, the money is gone.*

El jilguerito con pico de oro

from *Los amantes chasqueados* (1779)

[los amántes ʧaskeáðos]

Blas de Laserna
(1751–1816)

1
el xilɣeríto
El jilguerito
The little-linnet

2
kon píko ðe_óro
con pico de oro
with beak of gold

3
kánta sonóro
canta sonoro
sings sonorously

4
i tóðo _ es trinár
y todo _ es trinar.
and everything is singing.

5
krúθa la sélβa
Cruza la selva
He-crosses the grove

6
de ráma_en ráma
de rama en rama
from branch to branch,

7
ja la ke áma
y a la que ama
and for her whom he-loves

8
buskándo βa
buscando va.
looking he-is.

Poetic idea: "The little bird is happily singing and seeking his beloved."

This song is sung by the mischievous maid of a young woman who is being pursued by two foolish old men, referred to in the title, *The Duped Lovers*. The servant, who is playing an active role in ridiculing the men, has promised to arrange it so that they can hear the object of their love sing. Instead, she locks them in a dark closet and sings this charming song herself, imitating the style of her mistress.

Background: *Los amantes chasqueados* was a tonadilla for three voices, starring the beautiful singer/actress Maria Guerrero. *La Guerrera,* as she

was usually called, was not only a fine actress and singer but a virtuoso on the *salterio* or psaltery. This instrument, which was fashionable in Madrid in the late 1700s, had metallic strings which were struck with little wooden mallets to produce brilliant popping sounds. La Guerrera accompanied herself on the salterio while singing this charming minuet.

Although *"El jilguerito"* bears other European influences, such as the minuet style and the modified da capo format, it was felt to be Spanish because of the use of the salterio (which itself is Arabic in origin). Performed without benefit of this unique accompanying instrument however, the song still holds a great deal of charm and appeal.

Joaquín Nin did a setting of this song in the first volume of *Quatorze Airs anciens d' auteurs espagnols.*

Source: (1) *Teatro lírico español . . . ,* Vol. 2, Felipe Pedrell (La Coruña, 1898), pp. 30–34. Microfilm copy (Shelf No. 772), Library of Congress, Washington, D.C.

(2) Reprinted, omitting the final section, in: *"La Musique en Espagne,"* Rafael Mitjana in *Encyclopédie de la musique et dictionnaire du Conservatoire,* Part I, Vol. 4, Lavignac-Laurencie (Paris, 1920), pp. 2242–2244.

Original key: G Major. For soprano, violins, violas, cellos, flutes and salterio. The elaborate upper line of the accompaniment is the original salterio scoring. The salterio typically played a single line of music with a few accents of chords. The orchestra provided the harmonic structure and occasionally supported the salterio melody a third or sixth below.

Modest embellishments, suggesting the effect of trilling birds, have been given here by the editor.

*Signature of Blas de Lasema
on a legal document dated 1809.*

El jilguerito con pico de oro

Blas de Laserna

Blas de Laserna
Transcribed by Felipe Pedrell
Arranged for piano by Carol Mikkelsen

El jil - gue - ri - to   con pi - co

ⓐ Performed (Same in accompaniment)

Idiomatic translation: The little linnet with his

golden beak sings merrily, and everything else sings back.

From bough to bough he crosses the grove, looking for her whom he loves.

(b) Sing as two eighth notes as in accompaniment.

(c) Although the ornament is written as an acciaccatura, sing it as the first of four equal sixteenth notes.

(d) Play and sing ornaments quickly and before the beat.

e Sing quickly and before the beat.

Tirana del Trípili

Blas de Laserna
(1751–1816)

1
del   trípili   la tirána
Del   Trípili   la tirana
Of-the Trípili   the tirana

2
es la   ke mas ɣústo ða
es la   que más gusto da.
is the-one that more pleasure gives.

3
 dónde‿está‿éste soneθíʎo
¿Dónde está este sonecillo?
Where is   this little-tune?

4
toðítos pwéðen kaʎár
Toditos pueden callar.
Everyone can   be-silent.

5
trípili, trípili, trápala, trápala
Trípili, Trípili, Trápala, Trápala,
Trípili, Trípili, Trápala, Trápala,

6
késta   tirána se kántai̯ se βái̯la
que esta tirana se canta y se baila.
that this tirana they sing and they dance.

7
bái̯la ʧikíʎa,   kánta kon gráθja
Baila, chiquilla, canta con gracia,
Dance, girl,   sing   with grace,

8
tintiripín, tirána, tirána
Tintiririn, tirana, tirana.
Tintiririn, tirana, tirana.

9
dále ke ðále, xála ke xála
Dale, que dale, jala que jala.
Go-ahead,   keep-at-it.

10
ke me   róβas   el álma tirána.
¡Que me   robas   el alma tirana!
How from-me you-steal the soul, tirana!

Poetic idea: "Trípili, trípili, trápala, trápala, this tirana is sung and danced."

This dance-song with an untranslatable title is characterized by a nonsensical play on words. The refrain features words beginning with the letter "t." The *trípili* is an ancient type of dance-song. The expressions *"trápala"* and *"tintiririn"* are used in the refrain in the same way as the English "fa la la."

Line 9: *Dale que dale, jala que jala* are idiomatic expressions used to urge some one to keep doing something.

Background: *"Tirana del Trípili"* is attributed to Laserna, although its exact origin is not known. Certain songs from tonadillas became so popular that they circulated as independent songs both in their original form and in various arrangements. Many versions of this song exist, sometimes under the title *"El Trípili."* The version used in this edition is that found in *"La musique en Espagne"* by Rafael Mitjana.

This tirana became known all over Europe during the 1800s in part because the Italian composer Mercadante quoted it in the overture to his opera *I due Figaro* (1835). Later composers have also borrowed the song. Enrique Granados used it in his piano suite *Goyescas* and his opera of the same title to capture the spirit of Goya's Spain. Isaac Albéniz also used it in a piano piece entitled *Rondó brillante*. Joaquín Nin has a setting of it, entitled *"Tirana,"* in *Quatorze Airs anciens d'auteurs espagnols,* Vol. 2.

Sources: (1) *Echos d'Espagne,* P. Lacome & J. Puig y Alsubide (Paris, 1872), pp. 124–131.

(2) *"La Musique en Espagne,"* Rafael Mitjana in *Encyclopédie de la musique et dictionnaire du Conservatoire,* Part I, Vol. 4, Lavignac-Laurencie (Paris, 1920), pp. 2290, 2291. (The name of the transcriber is not known.)

(3) Melody only in: *The Music of Spain,* 2nd ed., Gilbert Chase (New York, 1959), p. 131, reprinted from: *La tonadilla escénica,* 3 vols., José Subirá (Madrid, 1928–30), transcription from the original score in the Municipal Library of Madrid.

(4) Reprinted in: "Spain," Gilbert Chase in *A History of Song,* ed., Denis Stevens (London, 1960), p. 387.

Original key unknown.

Tirana del Trípili

Attributed to Blas de Laserna

Del Trí - pi - li___ la ti - ra - na es la que más gus - to da.___

¿Don-de_es-tá_es-te so - ne - ci - llo?_ To - di - tos pue - den ca - llar._

Idiomatic translation: The tirana of the Trípili is the most amusing one. Where is that little tune?
Silence, everyone!

Tirana del Trípili ■ 47

(a) Sing acciaccatura quickly and before the beat.

Trípili, trápala, you can sing and you can dance this tirana. Dance, girl, dance with grace! Go ahead! Keep at it! You are stealing my soul, tirana.

Cuerpo bueno, alma divina

from *El criado fingido* (1779)
[el kɾiáðo finxíðo]

Manuel García
(1775–1832)

1
kwéɾpo bwéno álma ðiβína
Cuerpo bueno, alma divina,
Body   good,   soul   divine,

2
ke ðe fatíɣas me kwéstas
¡qué de fatigas me cuestas!
how many torments to-me you cost!

3
despjéɾta sjestás ðormíða
Despierta si estás dormida
Wake-up, if you-are asleep,

4
jalíβja por ðjós mis pénas
y alivia por Dios   mis penas.
and relieve, for God's-sake, my sorrows.

5
míɾa ke si no faʎéθko
Mira que si no fallezco,
See   that otherwise I-will-perish;

6
la péna néɣra me akáβa
la pena negra me acaba.
the sorrow dark   me kills.

7
tan sólo kon béɾte‿ aóɾa
Tan sólo con verte   ahora
If   only by seeing-you now

8
mis pesáɾes se‿akaβáɾan
mis pesares se acabaran
my torments — would-end.

9
ajai̯ ke fatíɣas
¡Ay, ay, qué fatigas!
Alas,   what torments!

10
ajai̯ ke ja‿ espíɾo.
¡Ay, ay, que ya espiro!
Alas,   that now I-am-dying!

Poetic idea: "How many torments you cost me! Wake up if you are asleep and relieve my sorrows."

This serenade is sung by a young student with a guitar, singing beneath the window of a beautiful woman whom he has until now loved from afar. It is from the tonadilla *The Supposed Servant,* the plot of which deals with the student's pretense of being a servant in order to be near the object of his love.

Line 9: *¡Ay, ay!* frequently appears repeated in song texts. In such a case the *y* between syllables is pronounced as the palatal fricative [ʝ], and not as the offglide of a diphthong.

Background: The young student expresses his love in the rhythm of a polo, described on page 6. Like the other polo in this book, *"El Contrabandista,"* this dance-song embodies the spirit of the Spanish musical idiom.

When Bizet set out to write *Carmen,* he decided not to go to Spain looking for local color. Instead, he requested Spanish songs from the Conservatory library to use as models of the Spanish style. One of these was *"Cuerpo bueno, . . ."* used as the basis of the exciting entr'acte that precedes Act IV of *Carmen.* Spanish music authority Gilbert Chase states that the music of this entr'acte reveals the real soul of the character of Carmen and of the opera itself and this music springs directly from the Andalusian cante jondo, described on page 6. The entr'acte borrows many features from the song, among them: the same key and meter (but not the same tempo!); the persistence of the dominant tone in the bass; a downward four-note scale that occurs prominently in the bass. From García's melodic 16th notes Bizet built an even more brilliant melody played by wind instruments in a high register. Most significant of all is a trait that García took from cante jondo: chromatic melodic phrases that end with a descent to a prolonged dominant tone. Bizet carries this trait so far that the entr'acte ends on an unresolved dominant chord.

The melodic interval of an augmented second, found in García's introduction and implied in the vocal melody as well (measure 16), is another feature of cante jondo that Bizet built into the fabric of his opera. The augmented second is prominent in Carmen's "Fate Theme," heard at crucial points in the opera.

For Bizet and his listeners the various traits of cante jondo symbolized gypsy life. Later scholars have debated whether cante jondo owed more to gypsy, Moorish, or Jewish influences.

Joaquín Nin made a setting of *"Cuerpo bueno, . . ."* entitled *"Polo"* in *Vingt Chants populaires españols,* Vol. 2.

Sources: (1) *Echos d'Espagne,* P. Lacome & J. Puig y Alsubide (Paris, 1872), pp. 78–82 (in C minor).

(2) *Cantos españoles,* 2nd ed., Eduardo Ocón (Málaga, 1888), pp. 62–64.

(3) Reprinted in: *"La musique en Espagne,"* Rafael Mitjana in *Encyclopédie de la musique et dictionnaire du Conservatoire,* Part I, Vol. 4, Lavignac-Laurencie (Paris, 1920), pp. 2296–2299.

Original key: D minor. For tenor, orchestra and guitar.

Cuerpo bueno, alma divina

Manuel García
Transcribed by Eduardo Ocón

Cuer-po bue-no, al - ma di - vi - na,_

_ ¡qué de fa - ti - gas me_ cues - - -

Idiomatic translation: Lovely figure, angelic soul, how much torment you are causing me!

Awake, if you are asleep, and, for the love of God, make my sorrow cease. See that otherwise I'll perish, killed by this dark sorrow! If I could see you now,

all my woes would end. Oh, what torments!

Oh, I am dying!

El contrabandista

from *El poeta calculista* (1805)

[el poéta kalkulísta]

Manuel García

(1775–1832)

ʤo soi̯ el kontraβandísta
1 **Yo soy el contrabandista**
I am the smuggler

i kámpo por mi respéto
2 **y campo por mi respeto,**
and fight for my respect,

a tóðos los ðesafío
3 **a todos los desafío**
to all them I-challenge

pwes a nádje tengo mjéðo
4 **pues a nadie tengo miedo.**
since to no-one I-have fear.

ajajai̯ xaléo, mutʃátʃas
5 **¡Ay, ay, ay, jaleo, muchachas!**
Hey, hurry-up, girls!

kjen me mérka ‿ alɣún ílo néɣro
6 **¿Quién me merca algún hilo negro?**
who from-me will-buy some thread black?

mi kaβáʎo‿está kansáðo
7 **Mi caballo está cansado,**
My horse is tired,

i jo me mártʃo korjéndo
8 **y yo me marcho corriendo.**
and I — leave running.

ajai̯ ke βjéne la rónda
9 **¡Ay, ay! que viene la ronda,**
Alas, that is-coming the patrol,

i se moβjó‿el tirotéo
10 **y se movió el tiroteo;**
and — began the shooting;

ajai̯ kaβaʎíto mío
11 **¡ay, ay, caballito mío,**
oh, dear-horse mine,

kaβáʎo mío karéto
12 **caballo mío careto!**
horse mine white-faced!

ai̯ xaléo ke nos kóxen
13 **¡Ay, jaleo, que nos cogen!**
Hurry up, that to-us they-are-catching-up.

ai̯ sákame ðéste ‿ apɾjéto
14 **¡Ay, sácame de este aprieto!**
Hey! get-me-out of this mess!

Poetic idea: "I am a smuggler and fight for my respect."

In this song a smuggler brags about his status saying that he fears no one, but as the night patrol approaches, firing at him, he asks his horse to get him out of the mess he is in. The smuggler's cry of *"jaleo"* is used both to urge a group of girls to hurry and buy his goods so that he can depart and also to urge his horse to run more quickly to hasten this departure.

This song was inserted into the tonadilla *The Calculating Poet.*

Line 1: [ʤ] occurs in Spanish as a variant of [j] at the beginning of an utterance or after a nasal. Ex.: ¡Yo! [ʤo], soy yo [soi̯ jo].

Line 6: *hilo negro* is the black silk thread that is used to sew mantillas.

Line 12: *Careto* is a horse which has a white face but its forehead and rest of the head is dark.

Background: García first sang his solo tonadilla *El poeta calculista* in Madrid in 1805. After he left Spain in 1809, he performed it also in Paris and other cities. It is not clear when he decided to include *"El contrabandista"* in these performances. During the Paris performances audiences were so overwhelmed that García had to repeat *"El contrabandista,"* accompanying himself on guitar, three times at each performance. These performances launched the idiomatic Spanish musical style around the world.

This song is a polo, described on page 6. García felt a kinship with this Andalusian genre and with the character of the smuggler. The song of the smuggler became a rallying cry of the Romantic movement. García's daughter Maria Malibran often sang it, performing it with as much verve and passion as did her father. It remained popular among the Parisian artist community in the early 1900s.

Malibran's singing of her father's famous song inspired Franz Liszt to compose *Rondeau fantastique sur un thème espagnol ('El contrabandista')* in 1836. That same year the writer George Sand, also inspired by Malibran's performance, wrote a novel, *Le Contrabandier,* which reiterated the theme of the free artist.

After the revival of the zarzuela in 1841, following a long period when that term was not used, Basilio Basili chose this uniquely 'Spanish' song to incorporate into his *El venorrillo de crespo.* Ernesto Halffter used the smuggler song in his operatic version of the free-spirited gypsy of Seville, Carmen (*La Muerte de Carmen,* 1926). Fernando Obrados composed an elaborate setting of the song for voice and piano, entitled *"Polo del contrabandista"* (*Canciones clásicas españolas, Vol. 3*). The text was translated into German by Emanuel Geibel and set to music by Robert Schumann as *"Der Kontrabandiste"* (Op. 74, No, 10). The text of the smuggler song was also used by Victor Hugo in his first novel, *Bug Jargal,* and by Federico García Lorca in *Mariana Pineda.*

Sources: (1) *Cantos españoles,* 2nd ed., Eduardo Ocón (Málaga, 1888), pp. 46–49.

(2) Reprinted in: "La musique en Espagne," Rafael Mitjana in *Encyclopédie de la musique et dictionnaire du Conservatoire,* Part I, Vol. 4, Lavignac-Laurencie (Paris, 1920), pp. 2293–2296.

Original key: G minor. A feature of the polo is the vacillation between tonic and dominant. The song ends on the dominant. For tenor and guitar.

El contrabandista

Manuel García
Transcription by Eduardo Ocón

Idiomatic translation: I am a smuggler and fight for my reputation.

pe - to;_____ a to - dos los de - sa - fí - o_____ pues a na -

die ten - go mie - do._____

¡Ay, ay, ay, ja - le - o, mu - cha - -

chas!_____ ¿Quién me mer - ca al - gún__ hi - lo_____ ne - gro?_____

I challenge everyone and fear no one. Hey girls, hurry up! Who wants to buy my black thread?

My horse is tired and I must get going. The patrol is approaching and the shooting just began. Run, my dear horse,

(a) Perform the acciaccatura quickly and before the beat.

run, my white-faced horse! Run, they are catching up with us! Get me out of this mess!

List of Works Consulted

Aunos, Don Eduardo and Don Julio Gomez: *El musico Blas de Laserna* (Corella, 1952).

Chase, Gilbert: *The Music of Spain* (New York, 1959).

———, "Spain," in *A History of Song* (New York, 1960).

Cockburn, Jacqueline and Richard Stokes: *The Spanish Song Companion* (London, 1992).

Cotarelo y Mori, Emilio: *Don Ramón de la Cruz y sus obras* (Madrid, 1899).

Hamilton, Mary Neal: *Music in Eighteenth Century Spain* (Urbana, 1937).

Katz, Israel J.: "Flamenco," in *The New Grove Dictionary of Music and Musicians,* Vol. 6 (London, 1980).

Lacome, P. and J. Puig y Alsubide: *Echos d'Espagne* (Paris, 1872).

Ladefoged, Peter: "Some Reflections on the IPA," in *Journal of Phonetics,* 18, 335–346 (1990).

Laparra, Raoul: *Bizet et L'Espagne* (Paris, 1935).

Mitjana, Rafael: *"La musique en Espagne,"* in *Encyclopédie de la musique et dictionnaire du Conservatoire,* part I, Vol. 4 (Paris, 1920).

Nin, Joaquín: *Quatorze Airs anciens d'auteurs espagnols,* 2 vols. (Paris, 1923).

Ocón, Eduardo: *Cantos españoles* (Málaga, 1874).

Pedrell, Felipe: *Cancionero musical popular español,* Vols. III and IV (Valls, 1918–22).

———, *Teatro lírico español anterior al siglo XIX,* 5 vols. (La Coruña, 1896–98).

Radomski, James: "García, Manuel," in *The New Grove Dictionary of Opera,* Vol. 2 (London, 1992).

Starkie, Walter: *Spain: A Musician's Journey through Time and Space,* 2 vols. (Geneva, 1958).

Stein, Louise K.: "Acis y Galatea," in *The New Grove Dictionary of Opera,* Vol. 1 (London, 1992).

Stevenson, Robert: "La Caramba," in *The New Grove Dictionary of Music and Musicians,* Vol. 3 (London, 1980).

———, "Spain," in *The New Grove Dictionary of Music and Musicians,* Vol. 17 (London, 1980).

Subirá, José: *La tonadilla escénica,* Vol. 1 (Madrid, 1928).

Trend, J.B., et al.: *"Cante hondo,"* in *The New Grove Dictionary of Music and Musicians,* Vol. 3 (London, 1980).

Two women of nobility whose attire attests the lasting popularity of the large hairbows associated with Caramba. The Duchess of Alba was one of the ladies who were ridiculed in a tonadilla written by Pablo Esteve and sung by Caramba.

Portrait of the Countess of Carpio, Marquesa de la Solana, *c. 1793,*
by Francisco Jose de Goya y Lucientes (1746–1828).
Oil on canvas, 181 x 122 cm.
Louvre, Paris, France/Bridgeman Art Library, London/New York.

The Duchess of Alba, *1795, by Francisco Jose de Goya y Lucientes (1746–1828).*
Oil on canvas, 194 x 130 cm.
Palacio de Liria, Madrid, Spain/Bridgeman Art Library, London/New York.

Singing Castillian

by René Aravena

The pronunciation of the songs included in this anthology follows the phonetic rules of Standard European Spanish. The phonetic transcription of the texts follows the directives of the International Phonetic Association, which is the organization which publishes the International Phonetic Alphabet. I have used the version approved by the association in 1993. The only instance in which I depart from these directives is in the marking of the primary stress of a word. The IPA uses the symbol ['] placed before the stresssed syllable; I prefer to use the symbol [´] placed over the vowel of the stressed syllable.

IPA	This book
emphatic [ɛmˈfætɪk]	emphatic [ɛmfǽtɪk]

The symbols [e] and [o] represent the written <e> and <o> respectively. For singing purposes the Spanish [e] is a sound between the closed English [e] of <bait> [beɪt][1] and the open [ɛ] of <bet> [bɛt]. Similarly, the Spanish [o] lies between the closed English [o] of <boat> [boʊt] and the open [ɔ] of <bought> [bɔt].

Diphthongs (combinations of a glide and a pure vowel) are notated according to the position of the glide: if the glides precede a vowel, the symbols [j] and [w] are used. If the glides follow a vowel, then the symbols [i̯] and [u̯] are used. Ex:

Glide Preceding a Vowel		Glide Following a Vowel	
viento	[bjénto]	veinte	[béi̯nte]
vianda	[bjánda]	vaina	[bái̯na]
viola	[bjóla]	boina	[bói̯na]
viuda	[bjúða]	muy	[mui̯]
cuita	[kwíta]	tiuque	[tíu̯ke]
cuete	[kwéte]	teutón	[teu̯tón]
cuatro	[kwátɾo]	taurino	[tau̯ríno]
cuota	[kwóta]	bou	[bou̯]

The coalescence of the last vowel of a word with the first vowel of an adjacent word into a single syllable is called *synalepha* and is characteristic of the Spanish language. The symbol [‿] is used to mark this feature when the vowels are different. When the vowels are the same, they are merged into one syllable.

Ex.: <lo alto> [lo‿alto], <se oye> [se‿oje], <la idea> [la‿iðea], <que esperanza> [kesperánθa], <la aldea> [laldéa], <lo ocultó> [lokultó].

Assimilation, the effect of one consonant on an adjacent one, does not occur in slow or moderate tempos in singing. It does occur in fast singing and speech. An example of assimilation in Spanish is the voicing of [s] into [z] before a voiced consonant; for example, the word <asno> is not pronounced [asno] but [azno] because of the voiced [n]. This occurs naturally and is not specific to the Spanish language. The same applies to the velarization of [n] into [ŋ] when followed by a velar consonant, that is, a consonant formed by contact of the back of the tongue against the soft palate. Ex.: *tengo* [teŋgo], *cinco* [siŋko]. This book's transcription for these words is: [tengo] and [sinko].

---

[1]To avoid confusion I use square brackets [ ] to enclose a phonetic transcription and angular brackets < > to enclose the written letters, words or phrases.

Ten Pitfalls to Avoid When Singing in Spanish

1. Never aspirate [p], [t] and [k]. Instead use the unaspirated sounds found in the words <spy>, <sty> and <sky> respectively.
2. Do not sing <o> and <e> like [oʊ] and [eɪ] respectively.
3. Avoid the tendency of using a *schwa* [ə], especially in unstressed syllables.
4. Do not use [b] or [g] every time you see a <b> or <g>. They are used only after a breath or a nasal consonant. Use [β] or [ɣ] everywhere else.
5. Do not use [d] every time you see a <d>. It is used only after a breath or after <n> or <l>. Use [ð] everywhere else.
6. Never use [v]. It does not exist in Spanish.
7. Never use a velarized [ɫ]. It does not exist in Spanish. Use the [l] of <leaf> instead.
8. Never use [h] instead of [x]. [h] does not exist in Standard Spanish.
9. Never use [ɹ] or [ɚ]. Use the tap [ɾ] or the trill [r] instead.
10. Never use [j] instead of [ʝ].

Recommended Books on Spanish Pronunciation

Dalbor, John B. *Spanish Pronunciation: Theory and Practice.* Holt, Rinehart & Winston. New York. 1969.

Hadlich, Roger L., James S. Holton, and Matías Montes. *A Drillbook of Spanish Pronunciation.* Harper & Row. New York. 1968.

Macpherson, I. R., *Spanish Phonology: Descriptive and Historical.* Manchester UP. Manchester. 197?.

Stockwell, Robert, and J. D. Bowen. *The Sounds of English and Spanish.* University of Chicago Press. Chicago. 1965.

Recommended Spanish/English Dictionary

Simon & Schuster's International Spanish Dictionary. 2nd ed. Macmillan. New York. 1997.

Key to the International Phonetic Alphabet for Castillian

Symbol	Example Words in Spanish		Example Words in English	
[a]	cata	[káta]	kite	[kʰaɪt]⁴
[e]	pena	[péna]	pain	[pʰeɪn]
[i]	tío	[tío]	tea	[tʰiː]
[o]	costa	[kósta]	coast	[kʰoʊst]
[u]	busto	[bústo]	boost	[bust]
[i̯]	bailo	[bái̯lo]	bylaw	[baɪlɔ]
[u̯]	pauta	[páu̯ta]	pout	[paʊt]
[j]	pie	[pje]	yes	[jɛs]
[w]	puente	[pwénte]	went	[wɛnt]
[p]	pan	[pan]	apt	[æpt]
[t]	tul	[tul]	sty	[staɪ]
[k]	quepa	[képa]	action	[ækʃən]
[b]	van	[ban]	ban	[bæn]
[d]	doce	[dóθe]	dozen	[dʌzən]
[g]	gas	[gas]	gas	[gæs]
[β]	lava	[láβa]	—	
[f]	flor	[flor̥]	flour	[flaʊɚ]
[θ]	ceno	[θéno]	thin	[θɪn]
[ð]	odre	[óðre]	other	[ʌðɚ]
[s]	sin	[sin]	sin	[sɪn]
[j̈]²	ayer	[aj̈ér̥]	—	
[x]	ajo	[áxo]	—	
[ɣ]	hago	[áɣo]	—	
[m]	más	[mas]	mass	[mæs]
[n]	no	[no]	no	[noʊ]
[ɲ]	niño	[níɲo]	—	
[l]	luz	[luθ]	lose	[luz]
[ʎ]	calle	[káʎe]	—	
[ɾ]	para	[páɾa]	pot o'tea	[pʰɒɾɒtʰiː]
[r]	parra	[pára]	—	
[r̥]	par	[par̥]³	—	
[tʃ]	hecho	[étʃo]	etch	[ɛtʃ]
[dʒ]	cónyuge	[kóndʒuxe]	jug	[dʒʌg]

---

² This symbol represents a voiced palatal slit fricative similar to the initial sound in the English word <yes> but produced with more actual and audible friction.

³ Unvoiced rolled /r/. Used only in word-final position.

⁴ The small [h] is used to mark the aspiration of /p/, /t/ and /k/, characteristic of the English language and totally absent in Spanish.